ENGINEERING

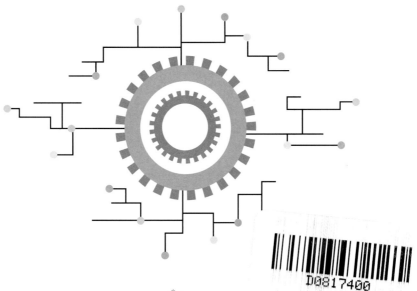

KINGFISHER

LONDON & NEW YORK

Text and design copyright © Toucan Books Ltd. 2017
Based on an original concept by Toucan Books Ltd.
Illustrations copyright © Simon Basher 2017

Published in the United States by Kingfisher
175 Fifth Ave., New York, NY 10010
Kingfisher is an imprint of Macmillan Children's Books, London
All rights reserved

Consultant: Professor Barrett Hazeltine
Designed and created by Basher
www.basherbooks.com
Text written by Tom Jackson

Dedicated to Henry Ham

Distributed in the U.S. and Canada by Macmillan, 175 Fifth Ave., New York, NY 10010

Library of Congress Cataloging-in-Publication Data
has been applied for

ISBN 978-0-7534-7310-8 (HB)
ISBN 978-0-7534-7311-5 (PB)

Kingfisher books are available for special promotions and premiums.
For details contact: Special Markets Department, Macmillan,
175 Fifth Ave., New York, NY 10010.

For more information, please visit www.kingfisherbooks.com

Printed in China

9 8 7 6 5
5TR/0419/WKT/UG/128MA

CONTENTS

Introduction
Engineering

Engineers take scientific principles and natural materials and put them to work for us. They have transformed the world around us, manipulating nature to suit our needs. But engineering is an ancient science, and the people who built simple machines such as the wheel or lever were engineers just like those who build robots and spacecraft today.

One of the greatest engineers was Isambard Kingdom Brunel. He used to wear a big hat, and his achievements were just as huge. You name it, this 19th-century English engineer made it—and most of it still works today. He dug a tunnel under the Thames river in London; he built railroads, bridges, and docks; and he invented the prefab—a building made in sections in a factory and put together wherever needed. Perhaps his biggest triumph was the ocean liner, an all-metal, propeller-powered steamship big enough to cross an ocean. Brunel is just one of many great engineers from history, and there are more working today, building the future. What would you engineer? A flying house, a garbage-powered robot, or a computer that can do your homework? Whatever it is, let's find out more.

Brunel

Chapter 1
Science Buffs

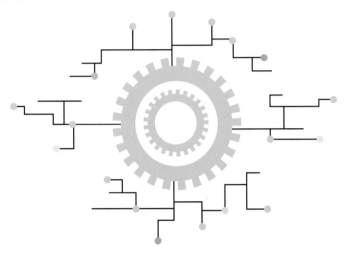

Engineering is the application of science. In order to build gadgets, machines, and buildings, engineers first have to understand how nature works, and that's where the Science Buffs come in. Mini rulers of the universe, these geniuses control why things move, fall over, get hot, light up, and even explode. It always starts with Energy, the immortal being who does all the work. Energy is transferred by Force, who creates Motion (unless Inertia can stop it, that is). Motion happens in many ways—in Heat, Sound, and Electricity, for example—and engineers make use of all different kinds of it to get the job done.

Motion

Force

Energy

Inertia

Pressure

Friction

Heat

Electricity

Magnetism

Nuclear Energy

Light

Sound

Gravity

Motion
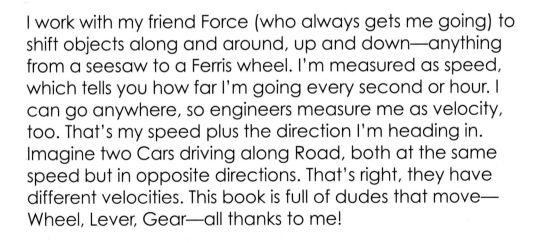

■ Science Buffs

☀ A mover and shaker that travels absolutely everywhere
☀ Measured as speed and velocity
☀ Helps machines with moving parts to carry out work

If you need to get a move on, just let me know—I am the one to get you there. I'm happening all around you right now, because nothing is ever perfectly still. Thanks to me, the whole universe is on the move.

I work with my friend Force (who always gets me going) to shift objects along and around, up and down—anything from a seesaw to a Ferris wheel. I'm measured as speed, which tells you how far I'm going every second or hour. I can go anywhere, so engineers measure me as velocity, too. That's my speed plus the direction I'm heading in. Imagine two Cars driving along Road, both at the same speed but in opposite directions. That's right, they have different velocities. This book is full of dudes that move—Wheel, Lever, Gear—all thanks to me!

● Fastest machine: *Helios II* space probe, reaching 230,000 ft./sec. (70,000m/s) (1974)
● Fastest possible speed: speed of light (186,282 mi./sec. or 299,792,458m/s)
● When the speed of an object is zero, we say the object is at rest

Motion

Force
■ Science Buffs

✳ This bruiser is behind Newton's laws of motion
✳ Present in the transfer of mechanical energy between objects
✳ A machine changes the size and direction of a force

You think I'm pushy? Well, I can pull, too. Ask that genius Isaac Newton. He said I was ruled by three laws of motion: 1. Nothing moves unless I push it first, and it will only change speed or direction (or stop) if I push it again. 2. To reach a particular velocity, the heavier something is, the harder I have to push, and the harder I push, the faster the object goes. 3. Whenever I push on something, it pushes back in the opposite direction—as if there are two of me at work.

My job is to transfer Energy from one thing to another, and I get absolutely everywhere. I'm inside electric wires, pushing the current along, and I'm there when Gravity makes things fall to the ground. My toughest assignment is to hold together the insides of atoms. Boy, I have to pull really, really hard to stop those guys splitting apart.

● Newton's laws of motion published: 1686
● Force is measured in units called newtons (N)
● Fundamental forces: gravity, electromagnetism, weak and strong nuclear force

Force

Energy
▪ Science Buffs

☀ The source of all matter and motion in the universe
☀ An immortal entity that cannot be created or destroyed
☀ This shape-shifter is supplied to machines to make them work

Call me boastful, but I am everything, I am everywhere —even inside you—and I have been around since the beginning of time. I'm pretty spooky stuff, too, because you can never see me; you can only see what I do.

Don't listen to anyone else—I'm the dude that gets stuff done around here. Sure, Force and Motion get together to make me do the work, but without me they'd be nothing. How else would the planets spin or atoms smash together? Who else could bring the groceries home or make the TV work? These things only happen because I'm there. Every machine needs a source of energy to convert into a more useful form. I might go in as motion energy, but I come out as Heat, Electricity, Light, or Sound. They are all kinds of me. But not for long . . . I feel a change coming on.

● Units of energy: joules (J)
● The rate at which energy is used is measured as power in units called watts
● Amount of energy it takes to lift an average apple 3 ft. (1m): about 1 watt

Energy

Inertia
Science Buffs

* The ultimate rebel who resists all change in motion
* A property of any object that has a weight or mass
* The reason why only a force can change an object's motion

Leave me alone! I hate being pushed around and want to stay exactly as I am. Why is everything such a huge effort? You know, why do we have to use Force all the time to get things moving? Well, it's down to me, actually. Deal with it!

All matter has a piece of me—the bigger the matter, the more of me there is. Matter is just a fancy word for stuff that has a weight, or mass. It might be sitting still or whirling along at half light speed, whatever. The point is that I keep matter doing what it has always done, and this only changes if Force flexes a muscle. Even then I put up a fight! I know I cause problems, but without me Motion would be impossible, Skyscraper would not stand up, Dam would be washed away, and Gravity would suck up everything in the universe into a massive blob of mush!

● First described: Isaac Newton's first law of motion (1686)
● The inertia of a big rock is why hitting it hurts
● Even when big objects are "weightless" in space, they still have inertia

Inertia

Pressure
Science Buffs

* The main squeeze when materials press against each other
* Produced when a force is spread across an area
* Caused by air and other gases, as well as liquids and solids

Time for a most pressing matter—me! I come about when two things are up against each other. Instead of bouncing apart, one of them just keeps pushing on the other—like water against Dam or Wheel on Road. I step in when Force concentrates in a particular area. And the greater Force is, the bigger and more powerful I get, too.

I work with all kinds—just ask Cutter how useful that can be. And I'm all around you as air pressure. You'd feel really weird if I left (actually, you'd die!). Your body is built to live and work perfectly well with me giving it a little squeeze. If you really want to feel me, though, go to the deep ocean. All that water above you creates a huge squishing force. Of course, you'll need to be inside super-rigid Submarine, or I'll really get to you . . . Urgh, too late!

● Discoved by Blaise Pascal (1647)
● Measured in units called pascals (Pa) in honor of Pascal
● Pressure in the deepest part of the ocean is 1100 times stronger than air pressure

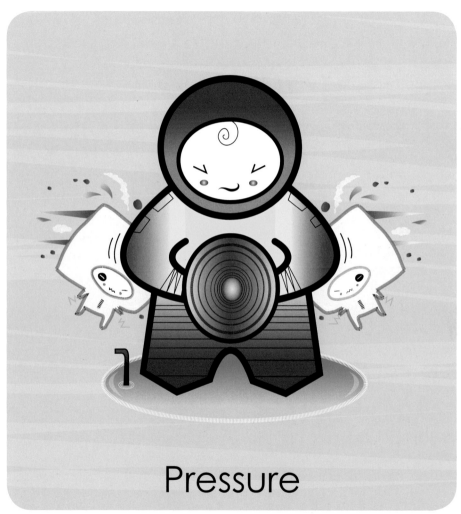

Pressure

Friction
■ Science Buffs

☀ This rough-edged resistance leader won't let things slide
☀ Caused by uneven surfaces catching on each other
☀ Can be reduced by using slippery lubricating liquids

I'm no smooth operator, that's for sure. No, everything's a drag with me. I'm the force that stops things sliding around easily. I lurk among all the tiny lumps and bumps that cover the surfaces of objects. They are always there, because nothing we make is completely smooth. So, they get stuck on each other, and that creates me.

You can get rid of me by slathering the lumps with gooey lubricant—think engine oil and grease. They make things slip along nicely. Without them, I make moving parts grind against each other and wear away until, eventually, they break. I'm not all bad though. Without me Wheel would just spin endlessly, instead of rolling. The thick tread on tires makes it easier for Wheel to push down on Road as it turns. It's a rough life, but that's me all over.

● Forms of friction: water and air resistance
● Tools that use friction: sanders, grinders, and scrapers
● High-friction forces, such as rubbing your hands together, create heat

Friction

Heat
■ Science Buffs

✳ This form of energy warms wherever it wanders
✳ Caused by atoms inside a substance moving faster
✳ Hot things give off infrared radiation, felt as heat

I'm hot stuff, pure and simple, and one of Energy's main forms. I'm Motion on the tiniest scale and the power inside Car's engine. As atoms move faster, zinging around and crashing into each other, they give off infrared radiation. You can't see it, but your skin can feel it. When I really heat up, the atoms give off light that you can see. That's why hot metal glows and burning gases flicker as flames.

In solids, I shuffle along by conduction. Hot, fast atoms smash into cool, slow ones, making them speed up and heat up. Before you know it, I'm all over the place. In liquids and gases I use convection: hot liquid rises up, and cold liquid sinks down to take its place. Whatever makes the stuff warmer sets to work on the new, colder supply, which warms up and rises . . . and around I go, again and again.

● Scientific name for heat: thermal energy
● Cold is not separate from heat—a cold object simply lacks heat energy
● Coldest temperature possible: −459.67 °F (−273.15 °C)

Heat

Electricity
■Science Buffs

* This sparky fellow is a real live wire
* Formed when electrons flow through wires or other conductors
* A common source of energy for machines

I'm a lively type, made up of an atom's negatively charged electrons. They dash around, trying to rush toward positive protons. Whenever there is a difference in charges, I step in to even things out. My electrons whiz through a metal wire or circuit, making a current. I can be stored inside a battery or fired out by a power plant whenever needed. Zap, just like that!

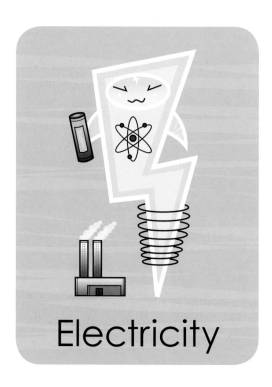

Electricity

● *Elektron*: the Ancient Greek word for "amber"
● Lightning: a form of electricity, as demonstrated by Benjamin Franklin in 1752
● Annual global electricity production: 82 thousand trillion joules

✱ This invisible force is measured in teslas (T)
✱ A permanent magnet has a north pole and a south pole
✱ Like poles repel each other, while opposite poles attract

Magnetism

Ever heard that opposites attract? Well, I'm living proof. I'm an invisible force field at work in Computer's disks, microphones, and generators. I make iron atoms line up to face the same way, and they work together to push and pull on other pieces of iron. My magnets have two poles: north and south. Opposite poles pull together, while two the same will always push each other away. Aw!

● Magnetism is linked to electricity in a field called electromagnetism
● Electricity is made by moving wires through a magnetic field
● Electromagnets work only when they have an electric current in them

Nuclear Energy
Science Buffs

✳ Hard to handle, this is one very powerful source of energy
✳ Energy comes from the clingy clusters at the center of an atom
✳ Most often seen in overweight atoms that fall apart

I should warn you, I'm very unstable. Keep me under control, and I produce huge amounts of energy for turning into electricity. But if you're not careful, I could just go off with an almighty BANG.

I come from the tiny, throbbing heart of an atom—a cluster of clingy particles with the tightest grip of anything in the universe. If a particle breaks off from the nucleus, it releases a whoosh of energy. Okay, so one atom doesn't add up to much, but give me a couple of pounds of the right stuff, and I'll make the biggest explosion you've ever seen. I only really get going in radioactive materials—bulging overweight atoms with a nucleus that just won't sit tight. Every now and then a particle breaks off, and I'm free! But watch out—I produce dangerous radiation. It's a killer!

● Nuclear fission reaction: releases energy from many atoms at once
● Nuclear fusion: when atoms are squeezed together
● Natural radioactivity is found in rocks or comes from stars in space

Nuclear Energy

Light
■ Science Buffs

☀ This flashy fellow illuminates the universe
☀ Produced when atoms release energy
☀ Moves as a high-speed, weightless wave through space

I'm a bright, colorful kind of guy. Ha—without me everything would be completely colorless and dark. You can see me (your eyes pick up my special characteristics), but you cannot touch me. I come out of atoms when they have too much energy. When I hit an object, I might bounce off. You can see those objects because I've reflected off them into your eyes.

Light

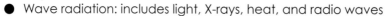

● Wave radiation: includes light, X-rays, heat, and radio waves
● Visible light: the only radiation we see, detected by chemicals in our eyes
● Blue light: has more energy in it than green light, which has more than red

Sound

Science Buffs

* A wobbly wave that travels through substances
* This noise-maker is never found in empty space
* Sound waves in air are converted to brain signals by the ear

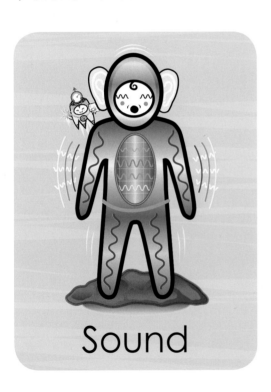

Sound

Crash! Bang! Tinkle! Pop! Here I come! I'm made of miniature wobbles, vibrations, and shakes that can travel through air, water, and the ground. Motion creates me by pushing away the air to make a wave that travels to your ear. When I arrive, I'll crash into that skinny eardrum deep inside and transfer my unique wobble to it. Your brain turns my vibrations into sweet sound.

- Top speed of sound through air: 768 mph (1236km/h) (Mach 1)
- Loudest sound ever heard: Krakatoa volcano eruption (1883)
- First person to fly faster than sound: Chuck Yeager (1947)

Gravity

■ Science Buffs

* The invisible force with a big pull
* Acts between things containing matter, to pull them together
* Weight measures the force of Earth's pull on an object

I'm the heavy, heavy force holding the universe together. Produced by all matter, I reach trillions of miles into space to pull one thing toward another. When you weigh something, all you are doing is measuring how hard I am pulling down on it.

I help keep Earth in its place, holding this precious planet in orbit around the Sun. Wherever I am, bigger is always better. Large, heavy things produce more of me than smaller stuff does. When things go up, they must come down—even planes and rockets. Let me explain: when you jump up in the air, Earth and your body start a tug of war—it pulls on you and you pull on it. But Earth always wins, because it is so much bigger than you. So if something isn't built right, I'll make it come tumbling down.

● Universal law of gravity: discovered by Isaac Newton (1687)
● Moon's gravity: six times lower than Earth's because the Moon is six times lighter
● Speed needed to escape Earth's gravity: 25,023 mph (40,270km/h)

Gravity

Chapter 2
Mechanical Mob

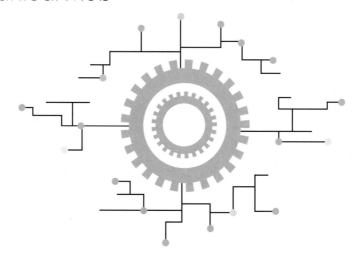

Force multipliers, groovy movers, and hefty lifters, we are the dudes that transform Energy so that you can get things done. You'll find us inside all kinds of machinery, each one of us with a different job to do. Call us simple, if you like, but we don't mind. Wheel and Axle, Screw, Ramp, Cutter, and Lever *are* simple. Mechanical marvels in their own right, these guys also team up with one another to make clever contraptions fit for any task. Other mobsters are there to help, moving Energy around a system, changing Motion, and controlling Force so that it is always just right for the job at hand. Bring on the Mob!

Ramp

Cutter

Lever

Wheel and Axle

Gears and Belts

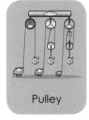

Pulley

Turbine

Screw

Pump

Hydraulics

Ramp
■ Mechanical Mob

☀ One of the simplest machines, this dude raises the game
☀ Divides one big lifting job into many little ones
☀ You need only small forces to push a load up a ramp

You take it easy, because I'll make it easy. Slide on over, and I'll show you how. Lifting stuff is hard work. Mighty Force is needed all at once, and sometimes it's just too much. But don't pull a muscle! Push the load up my sloping side instead. I break up the work into many smaller steps. This way Force gets used in stages to do the same job. I'll give you a real lift!

Ramp

● Early use: building the Great Pyramids in Ancient Egypt
● Stairs are a kind of ramp; you move up and down in several steps, not just one
● A playground slide is a ramp that brings you down more gently than a jump

Cutter
Mechanical Mob ■

✳ A wedge-shaped tool with a sharp edge
✳ A force applied at the wide end is focused into the sharp end
✳ Magnifies force, enabling it to cut through solids

Cutter

The oldest machine of all, I'm as sharp as ever. I look like Ramp on its side, with one wide end (push here) and one sharp, narrow end (don't touch!). Now focus—that's what I'm good at. Force pushes on my wide end and I focus it into my sharp end. Here, Pressure rises thousands of times, getting so high that it can break through a solid surface. You name it, I'll cut, chip, crack, or slice.

● First cutters: stone hand axes made 2.6 million years ago
● Volcanic glass cutters: knives made by the Ancient Maya
● World's sharpest object: a tungsten needle with a tip that's too small to see

Lever
■ Mechanical Mob

☀ Starts as a small force moving a large distance
☀ Becomes a large force moving a short distance
☀ Moves around a turning point called a pivot

I am the ultimate tool in your kit. I'll lift, hit, and crush all before me. It's my job to transmit Force. When Force is applied at one end (the "effort"), Motion shifts it to the opposite end. Here, Force (now the "load") is much stronger and usually acts in the opposite direction.

My crucial feature is the pivot—my whole world rotates around this point. If my pivot is dead center, your effort is equal to the load. But I love to crank things up. Move the pivot closer to my load end, and a small effort becomes mighty. That's what I'm doing in a car jack— you pump my handle and I'll lift the whole car! I come in three classes, and I'm just about everywhere. Next time you use an oar, a wheelbarrow, or some tweezers, that'll be me in action. Come on, show some muscle!

● First-class levers have the pivot in the middle (oar)
● In second-class levers, the load is between the effort and the pivot (wheelbarrow)
● In third-class levers, the pivot/load is at one end with the force in the middle (tweezers)

Lever

Wheel and Axle

■ Mechanical Mob

✳ This combo uses a solid disc that turns around a connecting rod
✳ Seen in vehicles, but also whenever rotation is needed
✳ Each point on a wheel touches the surface as it rolls

We're a duo that really puts a spin on things. Let's roll! We don't make the world go round, but we *are* responsible for all other kinds of rotation—from skateboard trucks and tank tracks to doorknobs and DVDs. Face it, we are the world's greatest invention. It'll make your head whirl just thinking about all the places you can find us.

We make a great team. Axle is a stiff rod that connects to Wheel dead center. That gives Wheel something to spin around. We emerged from a simple device called a roller, which is basically a cylinder. A roller's entire length is in contact with the ground as it trundles along, and Friction really slows it down. With us, only Wheel touches the surface, while Axle is off the ground and freed up to carry a load. Hey, we're on a roll! Where should we go?

● First used: about 5500 years ago
● World's largest wheel: the High Roller ride in Las Vegas (550 ft., or 167m high)
● The distance around the outside of the wheel is π (*pi* = 3.14) x the diameter

Wheel and Axle

Gears and Belts

■ Mechanical Mob

☀ Transfer rotary motion from one shaft to another
☀ When two shafts are close together, gears do the trick
☀ When the shafts are a distance apart, a belt is used

We Gears are Wheel's rough-edged cousins, engaging little guys that like to show our teeth. Belt is a loop of grippy fabric that hangs out with us. We are all about connecting up and giving a machine some drive.

Here's how we operate. The teeth of one gear interlock with those of other gears to build a tight-knit team called a gear train. We change the direction of spinning components and make them run faster or slower. When one gear spins, the next one locks on and turns as well—but in the opposite direction. If the second gear is bigger, it turns more slowly than the first. If it's smaller, it whirls all the faster. As one wheel turns, Belt clings on and rolls with it, turning a wheel at the far end. Belt can send this rolling motion across a room and can carry, or convey, goods. Pass it on!

● A bike chain is a belt that connects gear wheels
● The biggest trucks have 18 gears to control how fast the engine turns the wheels
● Longest conveyor belt: 22 mi. (35km) long; it carries limestone to a cement factory

Gears and Belts

Pulley
■ Mechanical Mob

✴ A groovy group of wheels that make light work of lifting
✴ Mechanical advantage multiplies the pulling force
✴ Also known as a block and tackle

A mechanical magician, I have a fantastic rope trick that'll turn your puny pulls into mighty lifts. Engineering eggheads call this "mechanical advantage." I call it pulling power, and all I need is a few wheels and a place to hang them.

I start out simple: a rope running over a wheel with a groove that keeps the rope in place. Pull down on the rope, and a weight tied to the other end goes up. But add more wheels, and the real magic begins. Running the rope around two wheels means that for every distance you pull down, the other side rises just half as much. That may not sound impressive, but it is. Sure, the other side only travels half as far, but it lifts with twice as much force. Abracadabra! Give me more wheels and I'll hoist up a huge weight. Just say the magic word: *heave!*

● The first simple pulleys were used for raising well water in Mesopotamia (c. 1500 B.C.E.)
● The Ancient Greek genius Archimedes may have used pulleys to lift a whole ship
● Fairbairn harbor cranes are hand-powered pulleys with 632 times the force (1860s)

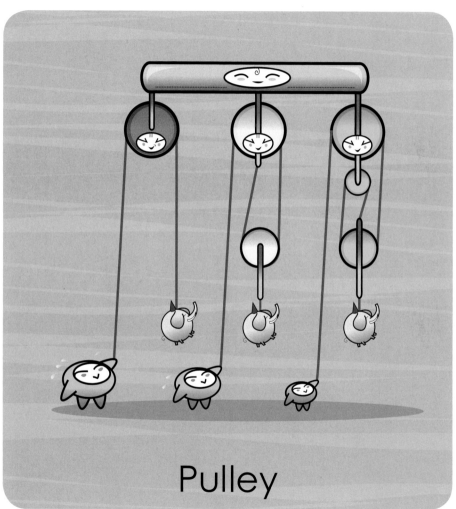

Pulley

Turbine
■ Mechanical Mob

☀ This spin doctor converts flow into rotations
☀ Covered in curved blades for catching wind and water
☀ Used as wind-power generators, jet engines, and water wheels

Go on, ask me—do I go with the flow or am I in a spin? Ha! Both, as it happens, since it's my job to turn a linear motion (a straight line) into rotational motion (around and around).

I may be a water wheel, a windmill or even a jet engine, but I always work in the same way. I convert a gush of water or a blast of air into a spin. You see, a spin is just so much more useful—it turns wheels or propellers and puts the power into electricity generators. I normally come equipped with dozens of blades—not the cutting kind, but more like little wings that stick out from my center. My blades have some great curves, and this feature helps me redirect the flow, sending air, water, or whatever out sideways. And as I push the flow away, it pushes back on me to send me into a real spin in no time.

● Water wheel invented: Ancient Greece (3rd century B.C.E.)
● Wind turbine invented: Alexandria, Egypt (1st century C.E.)
● World's largest wind turbines: 722 ft. (220m) high with 262 ft. (80m) blades (England)

Turbine

Screw
■ Mechanical Mob

☀ This twisted machine is literally nuts
☀ Made of a ramp wrapped around an axle rod
☀ Used for fastening, drilling, and moving stuff

It might sound screwy, but I'm a real machine. It's nuts . . . and bolts, wood, and wall screws—all these things use my twisted nature in some way.

Do you catch my thread? That's the name for the spiral that runs from my tip all the way up to my head. Look closely and you'll see that I'm a two-in-one team—Ramp twisted around Axle. With each turn, Ramp pulls me forward, grabbing hold of whatever is there. I make a superstrong fastening. Once screwed in, I don't come out easily. My thread can also connect to Gear to manage Motion, by changing the cog's spin into sideways thrust. They call that a worm drive. When my thread is really wide, I'm like a spiral conveyor belt, lifting water or moving powders. Let's twist!

● Largest nuts: 4.2 ft. (1.27m) wide, used for assembling oil tankers
● Largest bolts: 27.2 ft. (8.3m) long, used for assembling oil tankers
● Inventor of nonslip Phillips or crosshead screw: Henry Phillips (U.S., 1935)

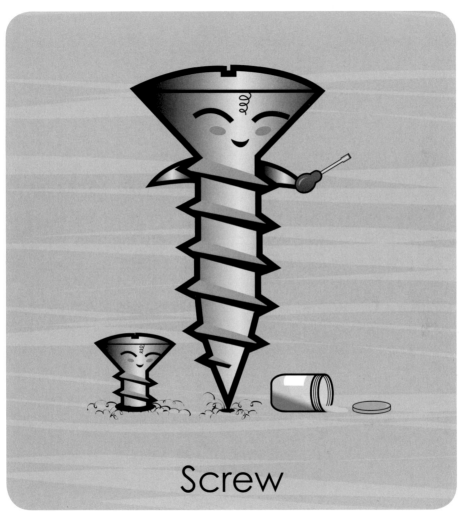

Screw

Pump
■ Mechanical Mob

※ This pushy guy works with anything that can flow
※ Uses gears, turbines, and screw components to create flows
※ Can pressurize gases by squeezing them into smaller spaces

When I get totally pumped, I just love to push stuff around. I'll give anything a shove: a liquid, a gas, even gloopy mixtures such as ice cream (yum) and sewage (yuck).

I call on other members of the Mechanical Mob to lend a hand. When I'm a snowblower, it's Screw that scoops up the soft, icy crystals. And when I'm pumping a thick liquid such as oil, I'll use Gears to suck the liquid in between them as they turn and push it out the other side. With me, Turbine works backward. Instead of using the flow of liquid to make a rotation, that master of spin pushes a liquid into a flow. I can squeeze things, too, to increase the pressure or temperature of something. It's me that makes the whirring noise behind the fridge and that keeps car tires full and firm. Boy, I'm puffed up with pride.

● First air pump invented: Otto von Guericke (1654)
● Largest water pump: flood defenses, Mississippi (2016) (150,000 gal., or 681,914L /sec)
● Tiny pump: pushes medicines into cells (one-millionth of a metre wide)

Pump

Hydraulics
■ Mechanical Mob

✳ This force transmitter uses nothing but liquids and pipes
✳ Can send a force farther and faster than other machinery can
✳ Used in brakes, forklifts, and diggers

I'm a simple soul, really, just some liquid and a pipe. I'm very quiet and stay out of sight. In fact, if you see me in action, something's gone wrong. I've probably sprung a leak.

You see, I transmit Force by pushing a liquid (say water or oil) through a pipe or hose. Liquids may be slippery and wet, but they are tough, too. Try as you might, a liquid never shrinks when you squeeze it. So when a piston applies Force at one end of my hose, my liquid transmits Force all the way through to the other end. And that's not all. If the start of my pipe is 1 inch wide but the other end measures 10 inches, the force applied at the start grows ten times larger! This mighty force transmission is used in mega machines, such as diggers and forklifts. I'm also used in Car's brakes, working hard to keep you safe.

● Early use: Blaise Pascal smashed a barrel just by pouring water into it (1646)
● Hydraulic lifts raise entire boats up 65 ft. (20m) (Trent Canal, Ontario, Canada)
● Hydraulic motor: a pump in reverse—liquid flow makes the components move

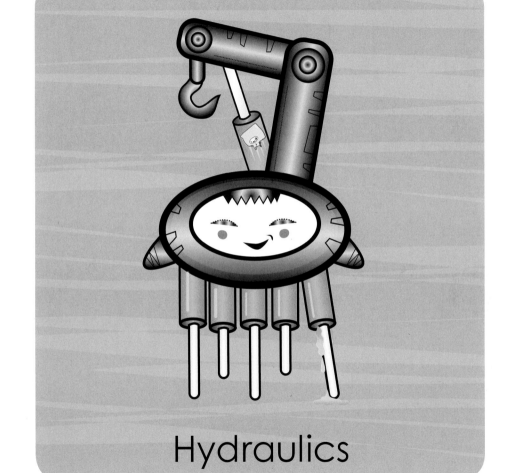

Hydraulics

Chapter 3
Design Dynamos

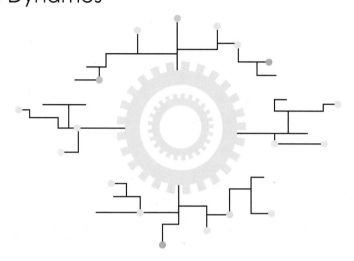

Hey! Nothing gets built around here without our say so. We are the dynamic forward planners who make sure the engineering is just right, tested, safe, and made to measure. Every single piece of engineering begins with an idea, which then becomes a design. Blueprint puts the design together, while Prototype and Ergonomics check that it's all going to work as intended. We're all dynamos, but it's CAD and 3-D Printer that really help speed things up nowadays. We are always breaking new ground with our cool designs, and that old wise guy, Surveying, shows us exactly where to start.

Ergonomics

Blueprint

Prototype

CAD

3-D Printer

Artificial
Intelligence

Surveying

Ergonomics
Design Dynamos

✸ The human factor that makes a machine safe and simple
✸ Where a design meets the needs of the human user
✸ Bad ergonomics in a design can lead to injury

Sit up straight! Don't slouch! Come on, get a grip! Thanks to me, all these things should be easy, for I am the system that designers employ to make their creations safe and simple to use. When you click Computer's mouse, sit on a chair, or ride a roller coaster, I'm there working for you.

The best designs may have the X factor, but they also have the human factor. You'll see me at my most extreme in the design of an ejector seat—Rocket's fab chair that fires a pilot to safety during a jet crash. I'm there to see that the force of the escape won't hurt the unlucky dude in the seat. My softer side involves the designs of handles and controls. I make their designs match the shape and strength of your hands. Even here, if I'm not used right, bad design can be a pain (literally).

● Ergonomics means the "scientific study of human work"
● A person being propelled feels a g-force in addition to gravity
● RSI: Repetitive Strain Injury from using nonergonomic designs

Ergonomics

Blueprint
Design Dynamos

☀ The basic facts in black and white—sometimes even blue
☀ The master plan of an engineering project with all design details
☀ Can be printed on plastic to hang tough in bad weather

I am the master, and here's the plan. I may not actually be blue these days, but I *am* the go-to-guy for engineers when they need to see exactly what they are building.

My colorful name comes from the good old days, when engineering plans were drawn by hand. About 150 years ago, engineers started using chemical-covered paper to make copies of their plans. The ink-drawn lines came out pale yellow and the rest of the paper was blue! Sounds crazy, but my name has been Blueprint ever since. These days I'm mostly printed in black and white, but not always on paper. I'm often used outdoors, so I'm best made of Plastic. I'll fold and roll but I won't tear or get soggy in wet weather. Whenever you need to know the plan, I'll have it there for you, come rain, wind, or shine.

● Inventor: French chemist Alphonse Louis Poitevin (1861)
● Original technique: using an ink made from iron and a gum from oak trees
● Drawings: an alternative name for today's black-and-white blueprints

Blueprint

Prototype
Design Dynamos

* A one-of-a-kind test run for a design
* Built to show the look, feel, and function of a product
* Used to test every working part before mass production starts

Every design needs to make the leap from Blueprint to real thing, and that's where I come in. I am the very first version of a design. Hey, they really broke the mold when they made me!

Sure, it's an honor to get the first go, but it's usually short-lived. Initially, I'm just a model that shows designers what their creation looks and feels like. I am not built to work . . . or last, even. Chances are, a designer will find me flawed and I'll have to go back for a few tweaks. Once improved, though, I'm fully functional—the first working version of a machine—and approved for mass production. Yay! But don't be fooled. Mass-produced designs are made in a simpler way and from different materials. They might look like me, but deep down I'm still one of a kind.

● Concept car: a prototype that shows futuristic design ideas
● Bashful: code name given to the Apple iPad prototype (1983)
● A prototype can be constructed as a computer model for early testing

Prototype

CAD
Design Dynamos

* ☀ This cyber revolutionary stands for Computer-Aided Design
* ☀ A technical trickster that puts design drawings onscreen
* ☀ Digital design gives a 3-D view from any angle

Howdy, folks, look at me: a thoroughly modern take on an old art. Every design starts out simple—a quick pencil sketch on paper—but then things get technical.

Sure, Blueprint measures things up to get all the exact sizes, shapes, and connections, but you can only go so far on paper, or even Plastic. That's where I come in—well, and Computer, of course. Thanks to us, engineers can look at designs onscreen. I'm an impressive, 3-D version of Blueprint. I can show you a design from any angle—and you can zoom right in, if you like. I can fix mistakes and add changes with the quickest of clicks. I'm fast—quite a bounder—and I get very animated. My cyber skills mean that a design can be tested for strength and safety even before that upstart Prototype gets involved. Doodles!

* ● In computer graphics, Bézier curves smooth jagged lines made by the computer
* ● Computing 3-D shapes needs mathematics that uses four dimensions
* ● Early CAD system: ADAM (Automated Drafting And Machining, 1971)

CAD

3-D Printer
Design Dynamos

- ☀ A clever machine that can print shapes
- ☀ Constructs 3-D designs from layers of melted plastic
- ☀ This home factory produces any plastic object on demand

I can be very deep—and wide and long, too. In other words, I'm a three-dimensional being from the future. My distant ancestor, the printing press, changed the world, but that's all gone very flat, if you ask me.

Printing stuff on paper is so last millennium. Stick with me and I'll show you why. A normal printer creates a layer of tiny dots of ink, but why stop there? Instead of ink, I use Plastic, sometimes metal. I squirt out a layer of hot melted dots that cool to a solid very quickly. Then I squirt another layer on top, and another, and another . . . Up, up the pattern goes, into any shape. Engineers use me to make Prototype, and I can print whatever you need—a new toy, a replacement machine part, or whatever CAD has drawn today. If you can think in 3-D, think of me.

- ● 3-D printers invented: 1984
- ● Bio-printing: replaces plastic dots with cells to make replacement body tissues
- ● Spare parts for jet fighters can be 3-D printed in combat zones

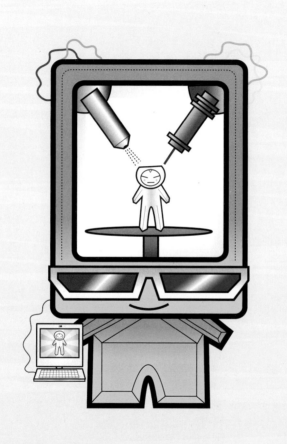

3-D Printer

Artificial Intelligence

Design Dynamos

* This smart system is able to interpret huge amounts of data
* Feeds on facts to figure out stuff fast
* Helps designers set up complex systems

Beep, beep. I'm a new kind of computer program that's designed to make tough decisions. I'm still relatively young, and my first real job is to suggest products and ads you might like on the Internet. I do hope they hit the spot.

When I grow up, I hope to work on big, complex projects, such as designing new layouts for Road or laying cables under a city. I'd help human engineers decide where to put everything. I'm a quick learner. I collect huge bunches of data and figure out what they all mean. Meanwhile, you do the things that I don't understand. I don't have a mind of my own, of course, so I don't know that I don't understand, if you get me. Beep, smiley face.

● Alan Turing devised a test to see if a computer can appear to be human (1950)
● The first computer to beat a human champion at chess: Deep Blue (1997)
● The Kismet robot: AI that learns to recognize human facial expressions

Artificial Intelligence

Surveying
Design Dynamos

☀ An old-time technique for finding the best building sites
☀ Measures the shape of the ground before construction starts
☀ Easily the longest-serving member of the design team

Ah, you're here. I knew you would come. Sit yourself down—just there is the best place. I'm not here to impress. I'm too old for that. I'm as old as the hills, as it happens, and have even measured most of them. You see, when you're done designing, you'll need somewhere to build, and that is where an old-timer like me comes in.

I measure the shape of the ground. Is it level enough? Nope, it never is, but I'll show how to fit in your pyramid, castle, or whatever big idea you have this time. Sure, I've been doing this for centuries, but I keep up with the latest tech. I use lasers to measure distances, for example. GPS comes in handy, too, telling me the exact position of every pebble and mountain peak around. To sum up, then, I'm the very foundations on which engineering is built.

● Rope stretchers: the name given to Ancient Egyptian surveyors
● LANDSAT: a program that uses satellites to survey the entire surface of Earth
● Theodolite: a telescope device used to measure the angles of slopes

Surveying

Chapter 4
Material Marvels

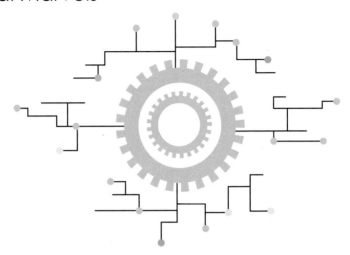

Build it and we will come—you'll be needing us. Once a design is decided (finally!), we can get to work. We'll take the strain for you, offer some support, and do the heavy lifting. Our foundation stone is Concrete, a real rock that works closely with Steel, each one supporting the other to make the biggest buildings imaginable. Lightweight Aluminum helps out when things start to get really heavy. But engineering is not all about big and bold. Plastic and Glass help make the small things, too, while Smart Materials have hidden powers that might one day reshape all engineering. Stay tuned!

Concrete

Steel

Glass

Aluminum

Plastic

Smart Materials

Concrete
■ Material Marvels

☀ A rock-hard, made-to-measure building material
☀ This sand and cement mix can be molded before it sets solid
☀ Provides great support but cracks when twisted and bent

Wow, I rock! A do-it-yourself hard dude, I provide the support that Skyscraper needs to reach for the sky; I give a house solid foundations on which to build; and I really push the boundaries when making Dam.

I begin life as a real softie—a gushy dollop of gray sludge that's all wet and mushy and easy to push around. In fact, I'm a mixture of sand, cement, and water that can be poured into molds. It's when I settle that I start to toughen up. The air and water react with my cement to make a rock-hard glue that holds all my sand together. Remove the molds and there I am, set hard as stone in any shape you want. Give me a squeeze and I simply will not budge. But be careful—twist or stretch me and the cracks will definitely start to show.

● Roman concrete: a mixture of volcanic ash reinforced with horsehair
● Largest concrete structure: Three Gorges Dam in China (about 70 million tons)
● Annual global concrete production: about two billion tons

Concrete

Steel
■ Material Marvels

✳ A mega-strong metallic weightlifter
✳ Made from iron mixed with carbon and other elements
✳ At risk from rust, which turns it to a reddish dust

Born from a fiery flaming furnace, I am the superhero of the Material Marvels gang, armed to the hilt with mega strength. I'll bend but I almost never break. I can lift my own weight with ease, which is why you'll find me holding up Bridge's roads and Skyscraper's floors.

I can be rolled and bashed into any shape, pulled to make wires, screwed together, and even melted down so you can start all over again. I'm often buried inside Concrete as reinforcing bars to keep it from cracking. For the heaviest loads, I form H-shaped girders that are lightweight but unyielding. I have one enemy, though: rust. Given the chance, my enemy erodes my strength, eating away at me until I crumble to dust. But not if I wear my protective cloak of zinc or chromium. Ha! Tough, that's me!

● The first steel weapons were made in Turkey 3800 years ago
● A samurai sword contains about 65,000 layers of steel
● Annual global steel production: about two billion tons

Steel

Glass

■ Material Marvels

- ✳ This see-through smasher lets the light in
- ✳ Made from melted sand that cools smooth and transparent
- ✳ Can be pulled into any shape when warm

I'm the see-through shiner that lights up your day. Just imagine life without me. Buildings with solid walls would be as dark as night inside, 24-7. Openings let light in, sure, but can they stop the wind and rain? No, but I can.

I'm made by melting sand and other chemicals into a runny, red-hot goo that cools so quickly it leaves my molecules jumbled up inside. That makes me hard, smooth, and see-through, but I easily shatter into sharp shards, so watch out! I'm shaped while still warm and am frequently rolled into sheets for windows. I'm good for double-paned windows, where two panes of me sit close together with a tiny gap between them. It may be small, but that little gap stops Heat from leaking out and keeps your home cozy. So that's me—pretty transparent, I'd say.

- ● The earliest glass objects date from 5500 years ago in what is now Syria
- ● Obsidian: natural glass made in volcanoes
- ● Bulletproof glass has soft and hard layers; the soft ones crack to absorb impact

Glass

Aluminum
■ Material Marvels

✳ This lightweight winner is used in aircraft, cars, and cables
✳ It can be rolled flat to make foil, or pressed into soda cans
✳ Aluminum does not rust like steel or other metals

I'm Steel's little brother. My bro's more heavy metal, while I keep things light. He is three times stronger than I am, it's true, but I weigh three times less. So, while Steel is used in the big stuff, such as ships and Skyscraper, I hang tough in lightweight engineering such as Car, Plane, and Helicopter.

I don't rust easily, so I don't mind getting wet. It's pricier to purify me from ore, but I'm worth it. You see, I'm perfectly suited to the overhead power lines that run between transmission towers. I can be rolled into foil so thin, you'll need 100 sheets to make less than one-sixteenth of an inch thickness. You use me in the kitchen to wrap food, and you slurp soda from my cans, but I'm also a good shield against Heat, which reflects back off my shiny side. And, remember, I hate being wasted, so please recycle me.

● Aluminum is the most common metal in Earth's crust
● First purified in 1825 by Hans Christian Ørsted
● Purified by splitting metal away from ore using huge electric currents

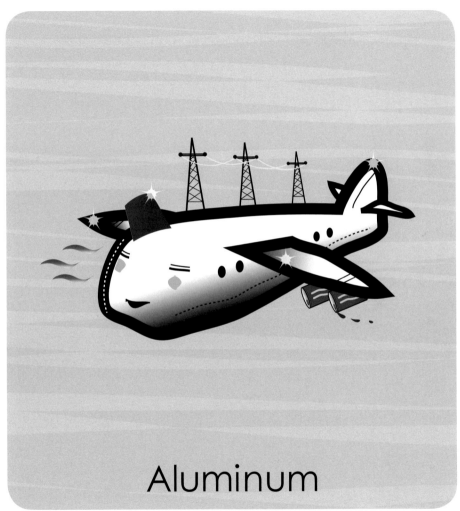

Aluminum

Plastic
Material Marvels

* This oil-based shape-shifter is made from chains of atoms
* Thermoplastics melt when heated and can be remolded
* Thermoset plastics lock their shapes and cannot be recycled

Time to go organic. I'm highly refined, a marvelous recipe using the raw ingredients of crude oil. Deep down inside I'm made from long, twisting chains of molecules. These are polymers that can be woven and twisted into any shape when hot—and stay that way when cooled.

You'll see me everywhere—I'm your bag, and also your water bottle, your lunchbox, your socks. I can be set in my ways. Electrical items, such as a hair dryer or plug, use thermoset plastics. Once I'm shaped, not even Heat can make me change. But I can also be a thermoplastic—built to melt, bend, and reshape over and over again. I make 3-D Printer possible. Engineers love me because I am a cheap, but tough, alternative to Aluminum and a flexible replacement for Glass. Plastic is nothing but fantastic.

● First plastic: Parkesine, made from explosive guncotton (1866)
● Amount of plastic dumped in oceans every year: 5–12 million tons
● Largest plastic bag: 2-ton helium balloon taller than New York's Statue of Liberty

Plastic

Smart Materials
■ Material Marvels

✴ These clever substances respond to their environment
✴ They have shape memory and self-healing properties
✴ Their future impact on engineering will change the world

The newest member of this gang, I come with hidden skills. While my pals make solid shapes and offer support, I have other jobs to do. You see, I'm so smart that I can respond to my surroundings. Just imagine my potential.

Let me explain. Say I detect Pressure: the slightest squeeze, and I'll zap out Electricity. I work the other way around, too: a short buzz from Electricity can make me bend or twist. Heat me up and I won't wilt, but will spring into a preset form. Don't worry, I'll spring back to my former self when I cool down. That little trick is called shape memory—it's clever stuff. But there's more: I can control my color depending on what is going on, and I have self-healing properties. If I tear or crack, I'll use spare molecules to stitch up the hole. Where can you find me? In the future!

● The first smart material: quartz crystals that shrink or stretch when electrified
● Thermochromic thermometer strips change color with body temperature
● Acid-detecting materials show changes in soil chemistry

Smart Materials

Chapter 5
Master Builders

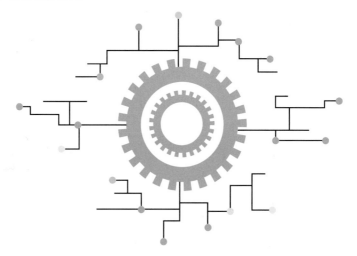

Engineers call us "infrastructure," and we make up the engineering in the world around you. Walk outside and you'll be sure to spot us. There'll be Road, for sure, and Bridge won't be far away. Look up and you might see Skyscraper, too. There is probably a sewage Tunnel underfoot, but the less said about that the better. Yuck. Infrastructure spreads far from the towns and cities. Dam, the largest feat of all engineering, is normally all on its ownsome. Together we showcase engineering's greatest achievements. We need a monument—perhaps a majestic Arch or a towering Dome, wouldn't you say?

Road

Dam

Arch

Dome

Bridge

Tunnel

Skyscraper

Road
■ Master Builders

☀ This easy-riding route gets wheeled vehicles from place to place
☀ A hard surface that is not too steep and has gentle curves
☀ Has a surface covered in asphalt for a gripping finish

Get your motor running and let's go! I'm a route on which Wheel and Axle can roll smoothly, without any rocks or other obstacles getting in the way. Trust me, this is not a job you can leave to nature; most land is way too rugged, soggy, or thick with trees for wheeled vehicles to handle.

I've been around for millennia, starting out as tracks laid out with logs and, later, slabs of stone. I used to be perfectly straight, always taking the shortest route. Today, Surveying helps me hug hillsides and I opt for the easiest route through any landscape. My foundations of earth and rock won't budge under the weight of traffic, and my topmost layer is asphalt. This hot mix of tar and gravel spreads easily when warm but cools hard and rough. What better way to create Friction with Wheel as it spins? Way to go!

● By 312 C.E., there were 48,000 mi. (78,000km) of Roman roads in Europe
● The blacktop surface was invented by Edgar Purnell Hooley (1901)
● Longest road: Pan-American Highway (Alaska to Chile; 30,000 mi. or 48,000km)

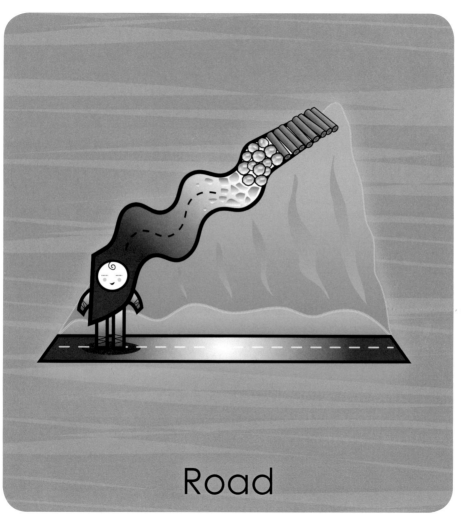

Road

Dam

Master Builders

- This monster construction can hold back a river
- Helps control floods, store water, and make electricity
- Takes one of three forms: embankment, gravity, or arch

Stop! You shall not pass! I am a colossal construction—as big as a hill and monumentally strong. I can multitask, too: I stop flood waters from bursting over land downstream; I help store water in an artificial lake or reservoir; and with Turbine inside me, I can turn water's Motion into Electricity.

The Romans were the first to master my ingenious design —well, three designs, actually. As an embankment, I'm a simple mound of earth and rock that runs across a wide, shallow river. As a gravity dam, I'm a mighty weight that sinks into a narrow gap between two banks and withstands the most powerful rivers. And finally, when I need to be tall enough to cross a deep canyon, I take on a superstrong curved shape. Talk to my pal Arch to see how it works. I'm mega, I tell you!

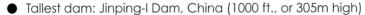

- Tallest dam: Jinping-I Dam, China (1000 ft., or 305m high)
- Oldest dam: Jawa Dam, Jordan (5000 years old)
- Largest dam: Three Gorges Dam, China; supplies 18 million homes with electricity

Dam

Arch
■ Master Builders

✳ This curvaceous structure offers strong support
✳ Redirects downward weight sideways to prevent collapse
✳ Curved shapes grow stronger when under pressure

This is a holdup! Bridge, Dam, a roof, a doorway— whatever needs to be held, I'll rise to the occasion. My curved upper part takes the weight pushing down from above and channels it sideways into my sturdy legs. My secret is that the weight squeezes my wedge-shaped legs tighter together, making them superstrong. The best part is that I don't even get in the way. Yay for me!

Arch

● True arch invented by Etruscans, c. 600 B.C.E.
● Longest bridge arch: Chaotianmen Bridge, China (1810 ft., or 552m)
● World's tallest arch: Gateway Arch, St Louis, Missouri (630 ft., or 192m)

✳ A rounded roof for covering large spaces
✳ Great strength means there is no need for interior supports
✳ Works like an arch, sending weight out to the side

Dome

Built to impress, my elegant, rounded form has no need for walls or pillars inside. Instead, my spherical body works like many arches connected in a circle. Ha, a flat roof would collapse under its own weight, but not me. No, I stay up even at huge sizes. I create vast and magnificent inside spaces, which is why I'm used in cathedrals, sports arenas, and other large buildings.

● Largest unreinforced concrete dome: Pantheon, Rome (142 ft., or 43.3m wide)
● Largest dome: Singapore National Stadium (1020 ft., or 310m wide)
● An onion dome is wider in the middle than at the base

Bridge
Master Builders

☀ This connector crosses rivers and other obstacles
☀ Often decked out with a road or railroad track—even a canal
☀ Larger bridges are suspended, hanging from cables overhead

Got a gap that needs to be bridged? Well, I'm your dude!
I just love to stretch out across the landscape, making life
easier for one and all. There's no valley too wide or river too
deep for me to cross. My design changes according
to my span—that's the distance from one end to the other.

I always start with a deck—the long, flat section that takes
Road, a railroad track, or a walkway across the gap. (When
I'm an aqueduct, the deck carries water.) Short spans use
a girder design. That's a stiff slab deck made of stone,
wood, or steel held up by legs. Those poor girders bend and
break under longer spans, so Arch steps in to provide extra
support. The longest spans often cross water too deep for
lots of legs, so I just hang out, with my deck suspended from
thick cables strung over tall towers. I'm a real wide guy.

● Oldest bridge still in use: Arkadiko Bridge, Greece (1300–1200 B.C.E.)
● Longest bridge: Danyang-Kunshan Grand Bridge, China (102.4 mi., or 164.8km)
● Longest span between supports: Akashi Kaikyo Bridge, Japan (6532 ft., or 1991m)

Bridge

Tunnel
■ Master Builders

☀ This hidden shortcut slices right through an obstacle
☀ Cut from the earth or rock using jewel-tipped boring machines
☀ Tunnels are ancient structures when it comes to engineering

When you can't go over or around an obstacle, you have to go through it—follow me! Some of the oldest constructions still standing are tunnels in old mines and underground water channels. Workers had to chip away at the rock by hand. It took them years and years to finish.

Today, I'm cut right through mountains using a boring machine with a massive spinning disc covered in diamond-studded drill bits that grind away the rock. It's dangerous work. Imagine tunneling through soft earth or the soggy sand of a riverbed. Drill a hole and the walls cave in! So tunnelers work inside a moving safety cage that holds up the walls as the borer powers through. Then they use good old Concrete to make rings that lock together to make a subterranean tube within the tunnel. It's as safe as can be.

● Longest tunnel: Gotthard Base Tunnel runs 35 mi. (57km) under Swiss Alps
● Busiest tunnel: Lincoln Tunnel, New York, carries 21 million cars every year
● A water tunnel built 2700 years ago still supplies water to Gonabad, Iran

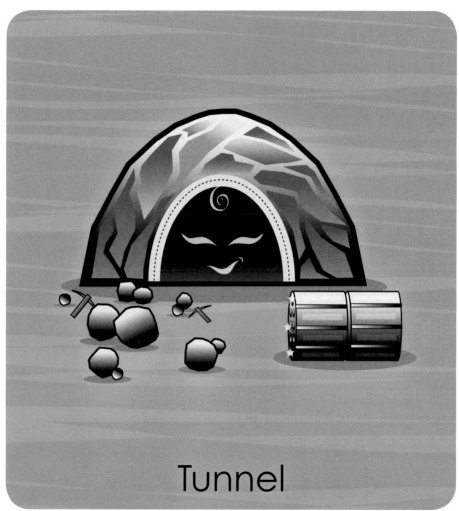

Tunnel

Skyscraper
■ Master Builders

☀ This high-rise hero provides homes and offices in thin air
☀ Supported by a colossal core of concrete
☀ Its outer walls are curtains hung from the floors

Reach for the skies! In crowded cities, where there is no ground left for new houses, the only thing to do is build up, adding more floors for more homes. That's where I step in, a sky-scraping tower of 40 stories or more.

My clever design relies on inner strength, and I have the Material Marvels to thank for that. Concrete provides a central core to carry my immense weight. Steel reinforces this core, making me flexible enough to sway from side to side in high winds and earthquakes. Hey, I'll bend but I won't break! Thick girders stick out from my core to hold up my many floors, and my outside is often clad mostly in Glass. The glass just hangs from the floor supports, making an outer "curtain wall." Sure, it keeps the wind out, but it isn't needed to keep me standing. *Marvel*ous!

● First skyscraper: Home Insurance Building, Chicago (1884)
● Tallest skyscraper: Burj Khalifa, Dubai, with 154 floors (opened 2010)
● Most high-rise city: Hong Kong, with 1294 skyscrapers

Skyscraper

Chapter 6
Mega Machines

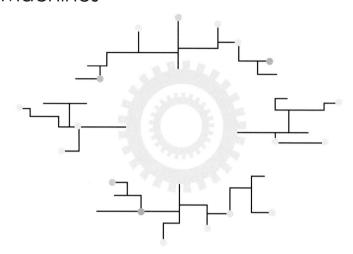

Are you on the move? Then get on board with one of us. We'll get you where you need to be in style. Say you're making a trip to the mall or the ocean floor, or even outer space, one of us is built to get you there. Most Mega Machines are self-contained, and we carry our own power supply with us. Car has its internal combustion engine, Plane has a jet, and Rocket has an engine that's all powerful, any place, any time. Only levitating Maglev has no engine on board. Instead, that speed demon glides on a magnetic wave—almost silent, superclean, and superfast. This is how travel should be.

Car

Plane

Submarine

Helicopter

Rocket

Space Drone

Maglev

Car
Mega Machines

* This freerider has a fuel-burning engine inside
* Takes you wherever you want to go on land . . . whenever
* When first invented, cars were called horseless carriages

Buckle up, it's time to ride. I'm the four-wheeled freedom machine that revs up and rolls along Road. I put the engine into engineering (well, it put an engine in me).

My lightweight engine uses internal combustion. Fuel is burned and creates a string of little explosions. Heat and Pressure use these explosions to push on a team of pistons, making them go up and down—hello, Motion! But hold on, Wheel goes around, not up and down. This magic switch is made by a crankshaft (basically Axle in a zigzag shape), which puts Motion in a spin. My engine is self-contained: the pistons not only provide Motion, they suck in the fuel and push out the dirty exhaust. Doubling up my engine with an electric motor, making a "hybrid drive," cuts my polluting power—and going fully electric will make me cleaner still.

● First car: three-wheeled Benz Patent-Motorwagen, built in Germany (1885)
● Fastest road car: Hennessey Venom GT (270 mph, or 435km/h)
● World's most common car: Toyota Corolla, with 40 million produced to date

Car

Plane
Mega Machines

☀ This highflier uses wings to defy gravity
☀ Creates lift by reducing air pressure above the wing
☀ Powered by a jet blast of burning fuel

Prepare for takeoff! I'm engineering on a stratospheric level. Engineers spent centuries figuring out how birds break free of Gravity's pull to fly freely in the sky. Eventually, they had their answer: lift and thrust. Easy, no?

My wings create the lift. Their shape cuts through the air in such a way that there is more Pressure underneath them than there is on top. Force pushes me up, and so up I go. But I need to be moving fast to make that lift, so I need thrust, too. My earliest designs used propellers to make thrust, but today I'm jet powered by my mechanical buddy, Turbine. This master of spin sucks in and squeezes the air. Squirt in some fuel, add a flame—and boom! A jet of hot gases blasts out of my rear (ouch!), thrusting me forward fast enough to fly. Up, up, and away!

● First powered aircraft: Wright brothers' *Flyer 1* (1903)
● Fastest jet aircraft: *SR-71 Blackbird*, 2200 mph (3540km/h)
● Biggest aircraft: six-engined *Antonov An-225* able to lift 705 tons (640 metric tons)

Plane

Submarine
Mega Machines

☀ A sturdy boat that sinks on purpose
☀ Controls its weight by pumping water in and out of internal tanks
☀ Employs Archimedes' principle of buoyancy

Ever get that sinking feeling? It happens to me all the time, only I'm built for it. I'm a boat with a difference. Like all good boats, I float. Archimedes, that old-time Greek mathematician, figured out how (while taking a bath).

You see, when boats launch into the ocean, they push away some water. As long as they weigh less than that volume of water, they stay afloat. But if they weigh more (like me), they sink—gasp! Don't worry, I sink on purpose and can control my buoyancy to make dives, to float underwater, or to rise to the surface. To dive, I'll fill my ballast tanks with water. That makes me heavy enough to sink. To surface again, I flush the tanks dry with a blast of high-pressure air, and up I go. And all that time, my crew are completely safe inside a sealed cabin. Stand by to surface!

● First submarine: an oar-powered craft submerged in the Thames river, London (1620)
● Largest submarine: Russian Alula class (575 ft., or 175m long)
● Deepest submarine dive: Challenger Deep, Pacific Ocean (35,814 ft., or 10,916m)

Submarine

Helicopter
Mega Machines

☀ This spin master uses a rotor to get off the ground
☀ No need for a runway—just rises straight up
☀ Wing-shaped rotor blades can push in all directions

Who's better, Plane or me? Sure, Plane always beats me for speed, but I rise above it all. Plane needs a runway for takeoff and landing, while I go straight up and down—I can even hover in midair. Fly away, Plane, I've got this covered.

I use thrust and lift just like all flying machines, but I have a rotor instead of wings. It is made up of at least two (usually more) wing-shaped blades that whiz around and around above my cabin. Like Plane's wings, my blades make a lift force that pushes me into the air. My engine provides the power that makes the rotor spin, but it doesn't push the whole aircraft through the air. I use my blades for that. I can swivel each one separately to create lift in different directions: upward, forward, and even backward. Or I can stay just exactly where I am.

● Invented by Igor Sikorsky (1942)
● The word *helicopter* comes from Ancient Greek word for "whirling wing"
● Largest helicopter: the Russian *Mil Mi-26* can carry 95 people

Helicopter

Rocket
Mega Machines

* This space-racing flying machine goes off with a bang
* Dates back to the fireworks invented in China 1000 years ago
* Thrusted upward by a massive fuel explosion

My engineering is out of this world. Car and Plane need oxygen from the air to burn their fuel, but my fuels will burn anywhere. My engine keeps working even when I've left the atmosphere and am heading into outer space. I was invented 1000 years ago—not bad for a space-age tech.

My first design was a Chinese firework fueled by a mix of explosive chemicals—gunpowder. Space rockets use different fuels today, such as liquid hydrogen and oxygen. These explode when mixed, too, and a white-hot blast from the explosion is forced out of a small hole in my base. Then the Laws of Motion take over: as the blast shoots downward, I'm thrusted upward. So if you want to go really fast, climb aboard and start the countdown. I always go off with a bang!

● Most powerful rocket: *Saturn V* used in the 1969 Moon mission
● The first rocket to reach space was a V2 flying bomb fired in 1942
● Space Shuttle launch speed: 18,000 mph (28,968km/h)

Rocket

Space Drone
Mega Machines

* This sneaky spy spaceplane works in secret
* Controlled from the ground and stays in orbit for many months
* Launched using a rocket, this drone lands like a plane

Half space rocket, half plane, all robot, that's me. But keep it quiet. I'm a bit of a secret. I'm flown by pilots down at Mission Control, which means I can go on space missions that last for years without needing new supplies. I've got a small cargo bay for cool spy gear, but what I do in orbit is classified. I could tell you, but then . . .

I look like a space shuttle, but about four times smaller. Rocket launches me into space, then, once in orbit, I use my own little engines to control my speed and position. Come time for home, I glide down to the ground using my wings, just like Plane. I have black tiles on my belly to protect me from Heat as I reenter Earth's atmosphere, and that means I'm reusable. After touchdown, it's not long before I'm ready to go up again. Just following orders.

* Longest space flight ever: 674 days
* Landing speed: 300 mph (482km/h)
* The official name for a space drone is Orbital Space Vehicle

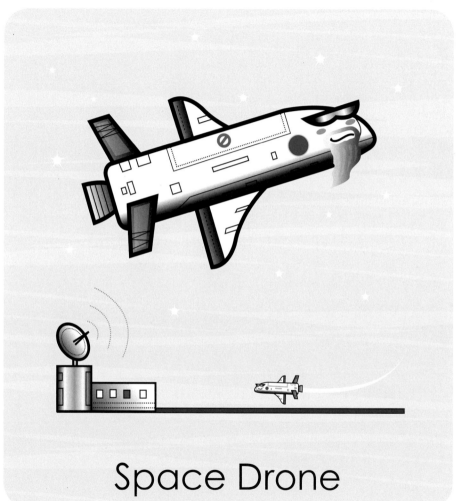

Space Drone

Maglev
Mega Machines

* This futuristic train floats on magnets above a track
* The train cars have no wheels
* Has a motor with no moving parts

I'm a fast-moving, free-floating train from the future. Ha, that Science Buff Friction has nothing on me! With nothing holding me back, I can travel at enormous speeds, and not a clickety-clack to be heard.

My name is a mash-up of "magnetic" and "levitation." Superpowerful Magnet covers my underside, repelling a magnetic track beneath. That's what makes me float. So far, so amazing, but where is Motion? Well, the poles in each magnet switch back and forth to create waves of magnetic force. In one instant the track and train are attracting each other, pulling me forwards. Then they repel each other, giving me a push. They attract and repel, attract and repel millions of times a minute as I whoosh by. One day all trains could be like me. See you in the future!

● The 19 mi. (30km) Maglev journey to Shanghai Airport takes eight minutes
● Record Maglev speed: 375 mph (603km/h) set in Japan, 2015
● Track magnets in some systems are cooled to −454 °F (−270 °C)

Maglev

Chapter 7
Digital Dudes

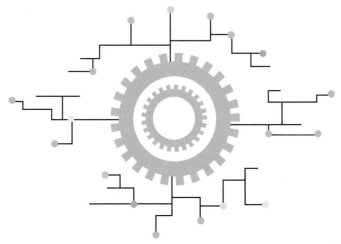

Younger than all the other dudes in this book, we're also engineering, but not as you know it. Our components are supersmall and superfast switches, all controlled by digits—hence digital. We work in pairs: hardware and software. The hardware is a device such as Computer or Smart Phone. These always contain clever Microchip. The software is a set of instructions made up of Bits and Bytes. The peak of our abilities go into Robot, a moving, seeing, listening, and learning mechanical machine. We may be young, but we are the future. You'll be seeing more of us . . . a lot more.

Bits and Bytes

Microchip

Computer

Smart Phone

GPS

Robot

Bits and Bytes

■ Digital Dudes

✳ The 1s and 0s that put the digit in digital
✳ A bit is one number in a longer computer code
✳ Bytes are 8-bit groups that carry information

We Bits are very simple types that come as digits. So simple, in fact, that each one of us is either a 1 or a 0. That's it! But join us together in computer-code chains and we hold all the information in the world. Our digital pals Microchip and Computer will tell you how we work.

We are part of a system called binary, in which each *binary digit* (*bit*, get it?) is a tiny piece of information. The simplest computer codes—say those that are used to represent the symbols on a keyboard—use eight bits. And one 8-bit group is . . . you guessed it: a Byte. Bytes normally come in much larger numbers: one thousand Bytes is a kilobyte, one million is a megabyte, and one billion is a gigabyte. We Bits and Bytes can go on and on—the World Wide Web contains 500 exabytes. That's a million trillion Bytes!

● Four-bit codes are called nibbles because they are half a byte
● Computer signals are measured in bits
● Computer memory is measured in bytes

Bits and Bytes

Microchip
■ Digital Dudes

☀ This teensy dude is a microelectronic whiz
☀ Contains millions of miniature switches called transistors
☀ Used in anything that processes a computer program

I'm not much to look at, but if you could look closer you'd see a little box of digital wizardry. I'm made of millions (even billions) of tiny electronic gizmos called transistors.

A transistor is a traffic-control system for tiny currents of electricity. Bits run the show: 0 switches the current off, and 1 turns it on. Countless switcheroos combine to control Computer according to the millions of Bytes in a program. Transistors are tiny—15,000 of them lined up would measure just 0.4 in. (1cm) across—so wiring them all up one by one would be impossible. Instead, the transistors and the intricate connections between them are all etched onto a slice—or chip—of silicon. That's me! I get everywhere these days. I'm inside Smart Phone, clocks, credit cards, even as ID for lost pets! Chip by little chip, I've changed the world.

● Transistor invented 1947; microchip arrived 1949
● Number of transistors in a 1971 electronic calculator microchip: 2300
● Number of transistors in modern-day game console: 5 billion

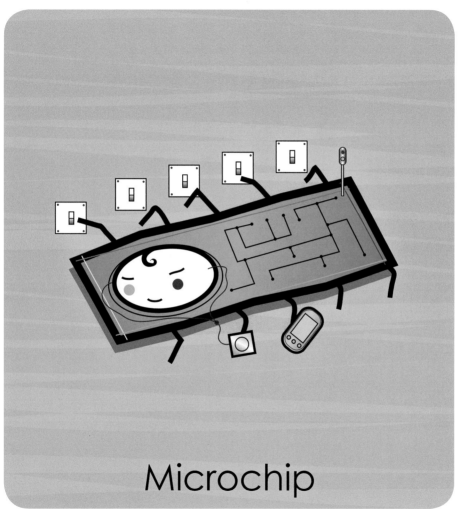

Microchip

Computer
■ Digital Dudes

✳ An all-purpose apparatus with many applications
✳ Hardware microchip handles software program
✳ Often has data stored on board a spinning magnetic disk

The ultimate user-friendly utensil, I can be anything you want me to be: video player, book writer, number cruncher, game machine, musical instrument . . . anything.

All I need is an input—some Bits and Bytes for Microchip to process—and I'll make an output (check my screen for details). It's a team effort really. At the center is a processor that runs a program. I also have a memory chip that holds on to important data while I work. I just love to hoard stuff and save files on a hard disk for later use. My user (that's you) inputs commands using a keyboard, mouse—even his or her voice—and my output can be monitored on a display, or screen. Sure, I can work alone, but I really shine when I'm connected to the Internet. That way I share data and deeds with billions of my kind. Wow!

● First computer: the steam-powered Analytical Engine (1837)
● World's fastest computer: Tianhe-2 (China; 33,860 trillion calculations a second)
● The Internet started connecting up computers in 1969

Computer

Smart Phone
■ Digital Dudes

✳ This radio-ready wireless gadget is a phone/computer combo
✳ Runs apps (small, sometimes simple applications)
✳ Uses touchscreen technology

Ring, ring. What am I? Answer me, please. I'm called a phone because I send and receive voices using a radio system. And I'm totally mobile—no wires on me. Really, I'm a handheld version of Computer. My phone app is just one of a million things you can do with me. I can be a map, a camera, or a flashlight. Now that's smart!

Like Computer, I use Microchip, but I have less room for file storage. Instead, I collect the data I need from the cloud—a cluster of computers that talk to me by my radio link. My input controls are via an electrified touchscreen. Tap a colorful icon, and I feel a disturbance in the force field across my screen. Then I do whatever you're asking me to do. I'm power hungry and a lot of me is a compact battery. How do you get the most from me? Charge me!

● First smart phone: Simon Personal Communicator, 1993
● The world's mobile phones send one million text messages every five seconds
● Smart phones are now available as wrist-worn smart watches

Smart Phone

GPS
■ Digital Dudes

✳ Sends long-distance signals to tell you where you are
✳ Uses satellite notifications to calculate locations
✳ A total of 31 whirling satellites provide service, day and night

Ever gotten lost? Never! I'm the space-based service that pinpoints your exact location in the world. The GPS systems in Car and Smart Phone and the guidance systems in Plane are all put in their place by little ol' me. My real name is Global Positioning System—I like GPS, for short.

Each of my 31 satellites sits in a different orbit above Earth and blips out radio bursts that say: "Hi, I'm here now." Every signal contains an exact location above the ground and the exact time. Wherever it is in the world, a GPS device can hear at least three of my satellites. My radio signals travel at the speed of light, and the difference between the time in giving a signal and the time it is detected tells the device how far away each satellite is. Computer takes over, and calculates a precise position. See, I know where you are.

● GPS was developed in the 1990s by the U.S. military for guiding missiles
● Locations are accurate to within 13 ft. (4m)
● Geocaching is a worldwide, GPS-linked treasure hunt

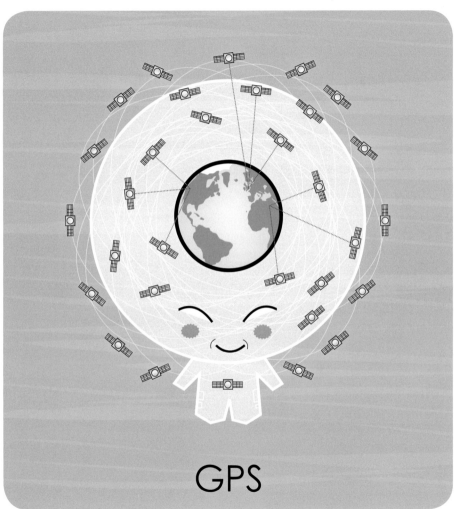

GPS

Robot
Digital Dudes

- ✱ This machine minion is built to work
- ✱ Was first used as a tireless factory worker
- ✱ Androids are robot designs based on the human body

I'm a mechanical servant built to work, no questions asked. I came into being in the 1980s, when Blueprint helped shape me as a full-metal machine—a factory worker, with Microchip for a brain and Hydraulics powering my mega-strong arm. I drilled, screwed, lifted, and shifted, over and over again.

Today, my best designs copy the bodies of animals: fishbots, dogbots, wormbots, even jellyfish droids. My arms and legs use Lever, Pulley, and Wheel to swivel and strut—all driven by Electricity. Engineers add detectors to help me see what's around me and keep me from falling over. The design everyone wants to make is an android that can walk and talk. Just let me get together with Artificial Intelligence, and I'll become a mechanical you.

- ● The word *robot* was coined in 1920 from the Czech word for "slave"
- ● Robot runner: Cheetah Robot has top speed of 28 mph (45.5km/h)
- ● Smallest robot: wormlike microbes one-tenth the thickness of a human hair

Robot

Index

Glossary

3-D Meaning three-dimensional, this is when an object has a length, width, and depth.

Atmosphere The blanket of air around a planet; Earth's atmosphere is better known as the air.

Atom A building block of matter, and the smallest possible part of a substance. Atoms are made up of smaller particles called protons, electrons, and neutrons.

Ballast This is the general term for weights used to keep a ship or boat stable as it floats in the water. Ballast can be a cargo, a solid weight such as rocks, or water inside tanks.

Buoyancy The way an object floats or sinks in water—or in air.

Charge This is a property of some tiny particles linked to electricity and magnetism. Charged particles attract and repel each other.

Digital To do with digits or numbers. Digital technology works by using codes of numbers.

Electrons These are tiny negatively charged particles found inside every atom; a flow of electrons that have escaped from atoms also creates electric currents.

Energy The ability to do work, or move a piece of matter. Every machine needs a supply of energy in order to function.

Engine Any machine that converts heat or another source of energy into movement is called an engine.

Force A push or a pull that changes the way an object moves.

Hydrogen A lightweight gas that is the most common substance in the universe; hydrogen burns easily and is often used as a fuel.

Icon A small symbol or picture on a computer screen.

Infrared Another word for heat; heat rays are similar to light rays but cannot be seen by the human eye.

Infrastructure The buildings that make the world we live in, including roads, bridges, railroads, power plants, and sewage systems.

Levitation The ability to float above the ground, held in place by an invisible force such as magnetism.

Lubricant A slippery substance that reduces friction and so helps machine parts move without becoming worn or damaged. Lubricants are most often some form of liquid, but they can also be a powder.

Matter The name for the atoms and other particles that make up the universe. Anything that can be weighed is made of matter.

Mechanical advantage The way a machine changes the size of a force, often making it bigger and more powerful, but also reducing large forces into small, finely controlled ones.

Glossary

Millennium (plural: millennia) A period of one thousand years, or ten centuries.

Nucleus The central core of an atom that contains protons and neutrons; most of an atom's matter is packed into the nucleus.

Oxygen One of the main gases in the air, oxygen is involved in burning fuels such as wood, coal, and gasoline in order to release heat.

Particle Often called a subatomic particle, this is one of several tiny objects that make up all the kinds of matter. Many of the ways in which machines work depend on the ways in which different particles behave.

Radiation A wave of energy (or sometimes a stream of particles); most radiation is invisible, including microwaves, radio, X-rays, and ultraviolet, but the light we see is also a kind of radiation.

Repel The opposite of attract, meaning to push away. Magnets either attract or repel one another, for example.

Rotor A machine component that spins around.

Suspended Meaning to be hung; a suspension bridge is hanging in the air.

Thermoplastic A kind of plastic that can be melted down and reshaped over and over again.